Building Tables on Tables
A BOOK ABOUT MULTIPLICATION

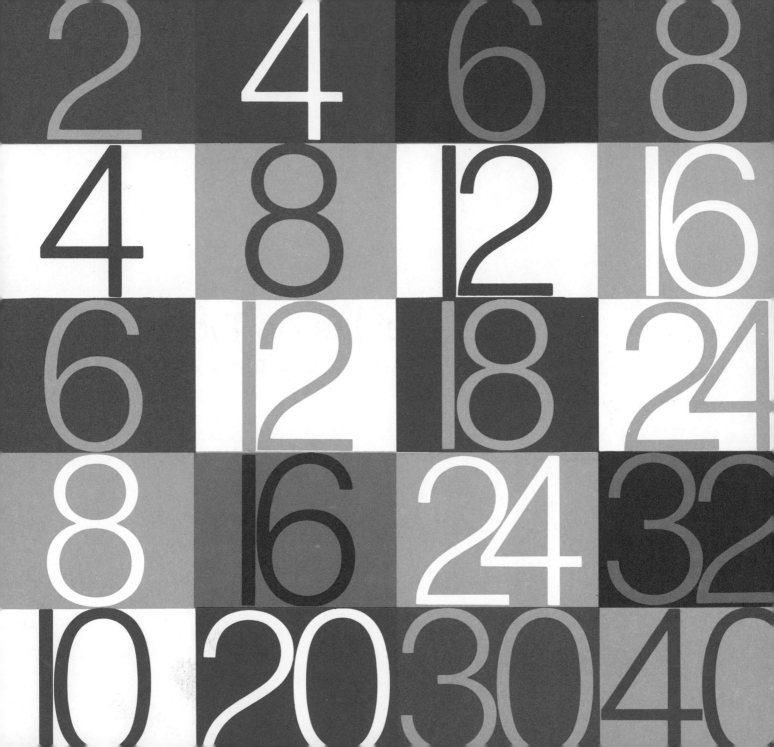

10 12 14 16

20 32

30 48

BUILDING
TABLES
ON TABLES

A BOOK ABOUT MULTIPLICATION

By
John V. Trivett

Illustrated by
Giulio Maestro

40 64

Thomas Y. Crowell Company • New York

50 60 70 80

YOUNG MATH BOOKS

Edited by Dr. Max Beberman, Director of the Committee on
School Mathematics Projects, University of Illinois

Copyright © 1975 by John V. Trivett, Illustrations copyright © 1975 by Giulio Maestro

Library of Congress Cataloging in Publication Data   Trivett, John V. Building tables on tables.   SUMMARY: Easy games help the reader learn the basic structure and principles of the multiplication tables. 1. Multiplication—Juv. lit. 2. Multiplication—Tables—Juv. lit. [1. Multiplication] I. Maestro, Giulio, illus. II. Title   QA115.T76   513'.2   74-11263   ISBN 0-690-00593-8   ISBN 0-690-00600-4 (lib. bdg.)

1 2 3 4 5 6 7 8 9 10

9-25-75 *New Method* 4.54

Building Tables on Tables
A BOOK ABOUT MULTIPLICATION

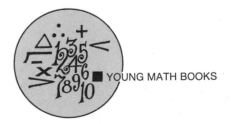

YOUNG MATH BOOKS

"What is three times four?"
You have often heard questions like this—
from teachers, parents, aunts and uncles!

If you say "twelve," they are pleased. Any other answer, and you may hear: "You don't know your multiplication tables!"

Play this game with your aunt or uncle or a neighbor—someone who doesn't know what you do in class at school.

GAME   Place four stones on a table.
(Or counters or buttons will do.)
Put another four with them.
Then another four.
How many is that altogether?

You have three sets, each of four stones: three times four stones.

We write **3 × 4**, and say "three times four." You could also say you have "four plus four plus four" stones; and write **4 + 4 + 4**.

Move one of the stones from one set to another.
You could now say "three plus five plus four"
stones.

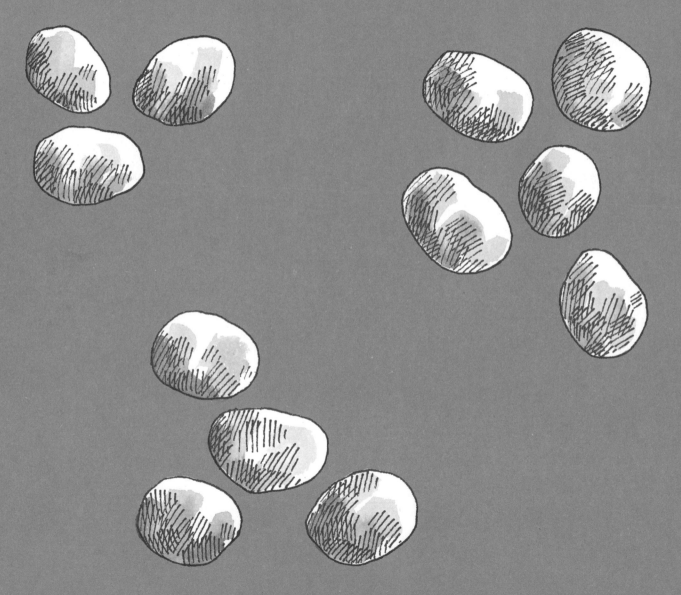

Tell your aunt or uncle that every name so far—**3 × 4**, **4 + 4 + 4**, and **3 + 5 + 4**—is a good answer to "What is three times four?"

They are all names for **12**.

See if they can find other names for **12** by moving stones. You can even show how to begin with fourteen stones and take away two of them to get **12**. That is written **14 − 2** ("fourteen minus two").

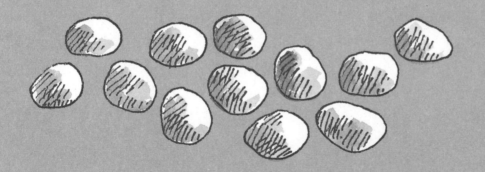

Make up lots of names for **12**. You can use plus signs (**+**), minus signs (**−**), and multiplication, or times, signs (**×**).

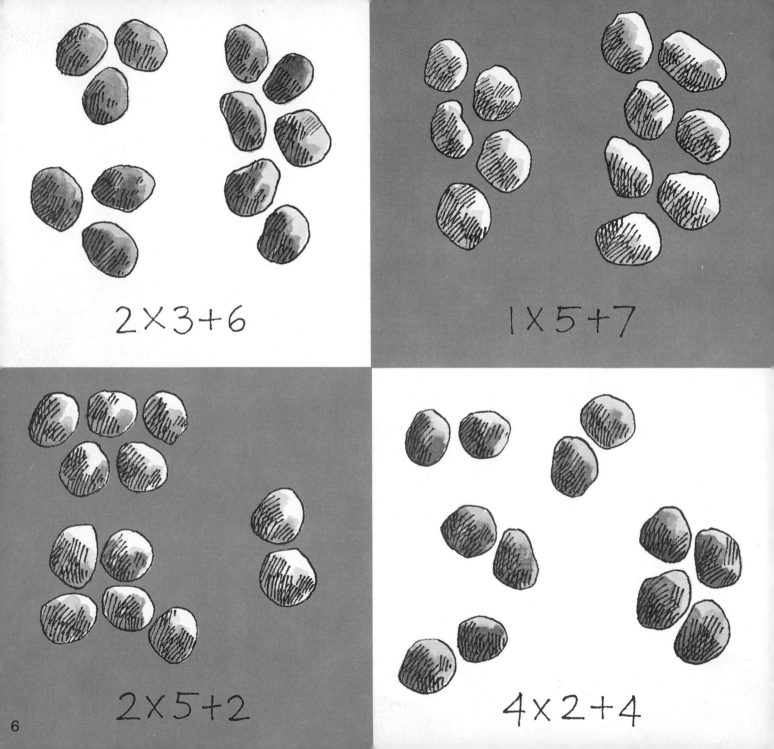

2 X 3 + 6

1 X 5 + 7

2 X 5 + 2

4 X 2 + 4

6

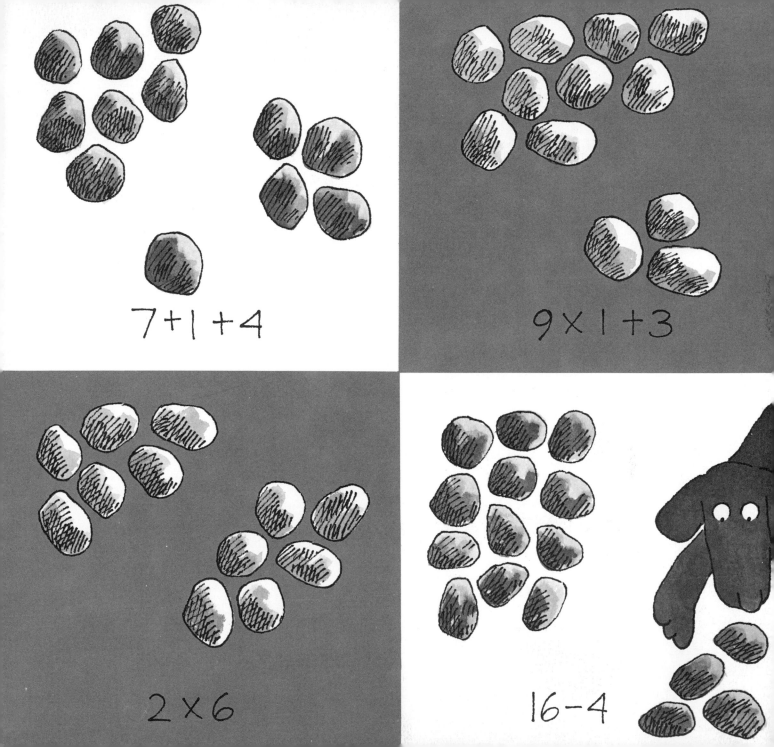

7+1+4

9×1+3

2×6

16-4

Suppose you want to write another name for **3 × 4**.

You could write **I + I + I** instead of **3**.

That gives **I + I + I × 4** instead of **3 × 4** —though it is easier on the eye if we draw a ring around **I + I + I**:

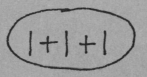

For short, we can write

$$3 \times 4 \longrightarrow \underbrace{(I+I+I)} \times 4$$

and read it, "three times four leads to one plus one plus one times four."

But **3 × 4** can also lead to $(1+2) \times 4$: so

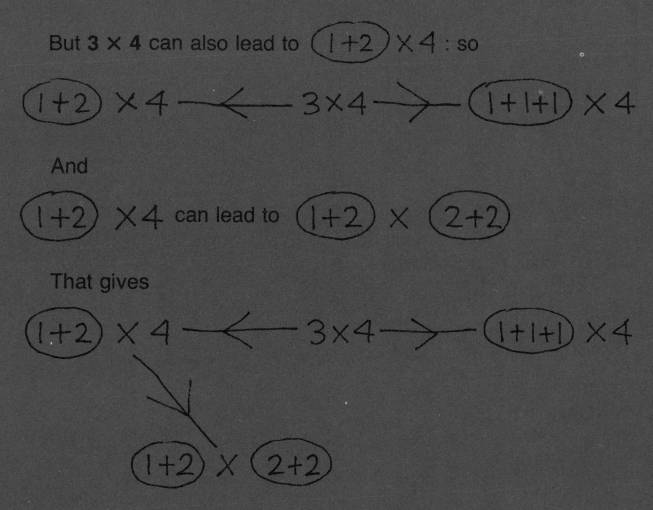

$(1+2) \times 4 \longleftarrow 3 \times 4 \longrightarrow (1+1+1) \times 4$

And

$(1+2) \times 4$ can lead to $(1+2) \times (2+2)$

That gives

$(1+2) \times 4 \longleftarrow 3 \times 4 \longrightarrow (1+1+1) \times 4$

$(1+2) \times (2+2)$

The arrows are drawn anywhere there is room
on the paper, from one number name to another
that you think of.

Does the drawing begin to look like a
spider's web?

Copy the following WEB onto paper.

Then add to it by making up other names and drawing the arrows.

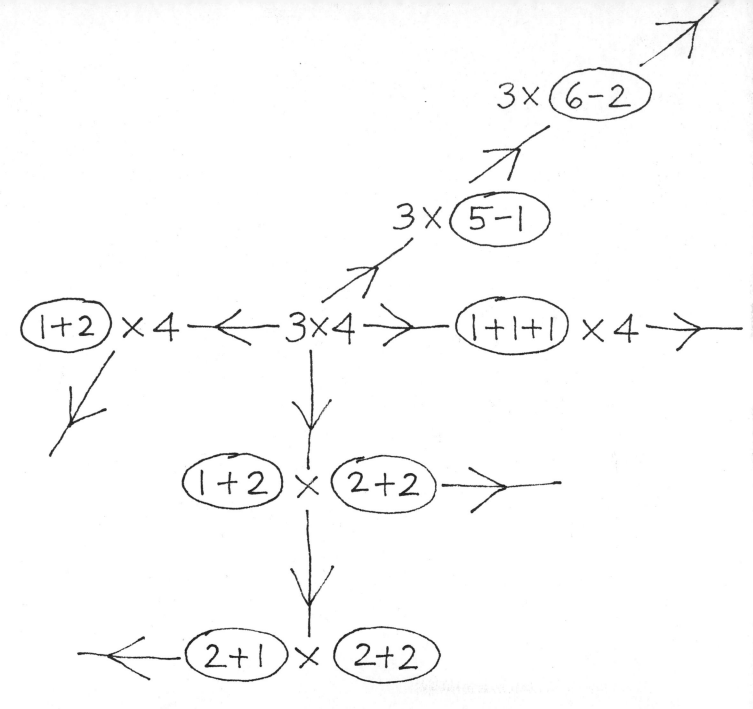

11

A name like **3 × 4**, using a ×, is called a PRODUCT.

12 is the COMMON NAME for **3 × 4**.

(**1 + 1 + 1**) × **4** is not a common name for **12**.

5 × 7, **7 × 2**, **2 × 3**, are other products. Write some others.

Then write the common name for each, on your own paper. If you need them, use the stones. If some of the common names are too hard, write other names which are not common.

Product	Not Common Name	Common Name
3×4	$4 + 4 + 4$	12
2×7	$7 + 7$	14
8×3	$3 + 3 + 3 + 3 + 12$	24
5×10	_____	__
6×2	_____	__
7×6	_____	__

Product	Not Common Name	Common Name
7 X 3	3 + 3 + 15	21

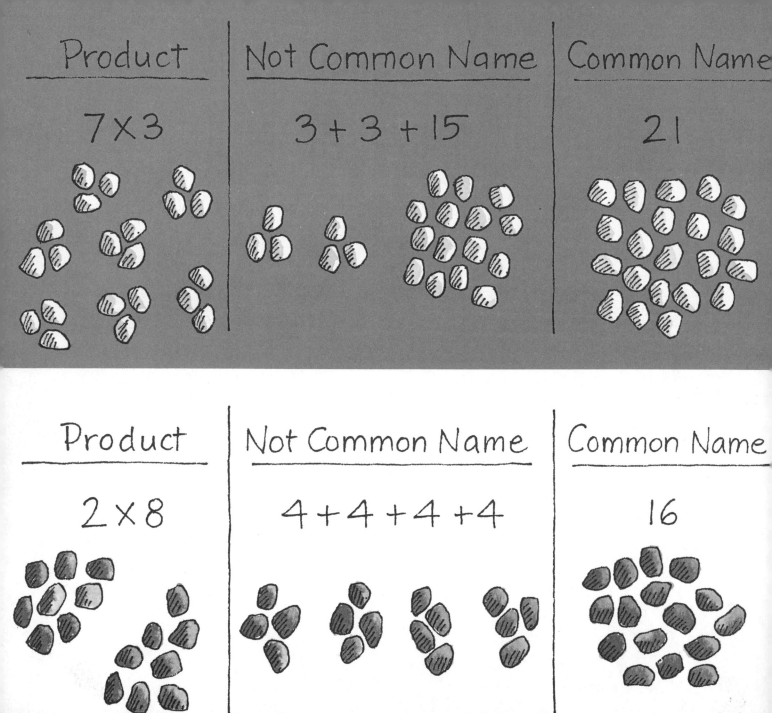

Product	Not Common Name	Common Name
2 X 8	4 + 4 + 4 + 4	16

Product	Not Common Name	Common Name
6 X 4	6 + 6 + 6 + 6	24

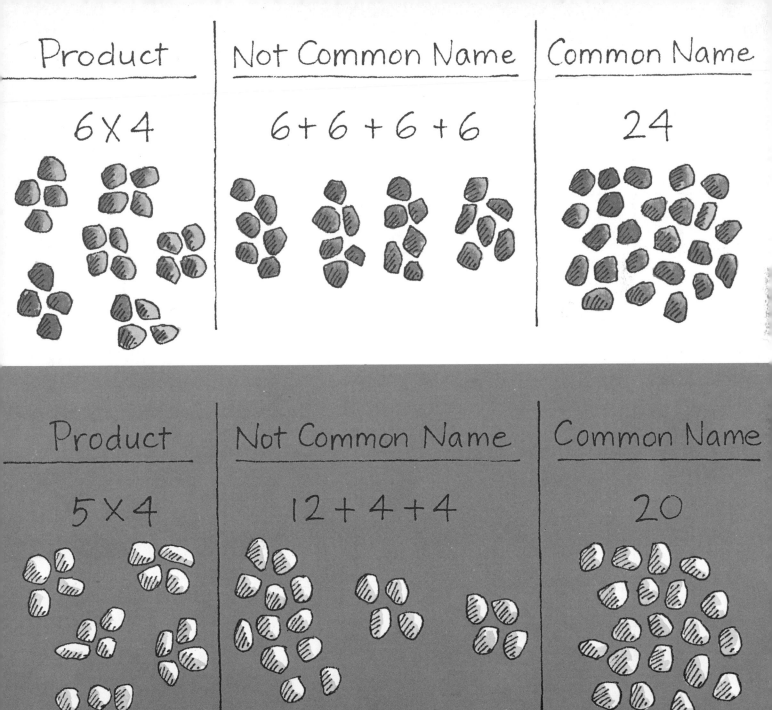

Product	Not Common Name	Common Name
5 X 4	12 + 4 + 4	20

15

GAME   Make a chart like this. (You can copy it.)

X	1	2	3	4	5
1	1×1	1×2	1×3	1×4	1×5
2	2×1	2×2	2×3	2×4	2×5
3	3×1	3×2	3×3	3×4	3×5
4	4×1	4×2	4×3	4×4	4×5
5	5×1	5×2	5×3	5×4	5×5

Erase each product in the chart and write its common name instead.

When it is filled with common names, the chart is a MULTIPLICATION TABLE.

Anyone can make his own multiplication table. He sits at a wooden table, moves stones, and writes the common names in a chart!

Here is another **GAME**.

From the multiplication table, you will see that
4 × 3 has the same common name as **3 × 4**, its
REVERSE. **2 × 5** is the reverse of **5 × 2**; they both
equal **10**.

Find some other reverses.

X	1	2	3	4	5
1	1	2	3	4	5
2	2	4	6	8	10
3	3	6	9	12	15
4	4	8	12	16	20
5	5	10	15	20	25

A change from **3 × 4** to (**1 + 1 + 1**) **× 4** is
a SUBSTITUTION—just as a substitute in school is
one teacher instead of another.

Reverses and substitutions can be used
together in a web game.

$$3 \times 4 \longrightarrow 3 \times (5 - 1)$$

Let us say a black arrow
means substitution.

$$3 \times 4 \longrightarrow 4 \times 3$$

Let us say a red arrow
means reverse.

Copy this web.

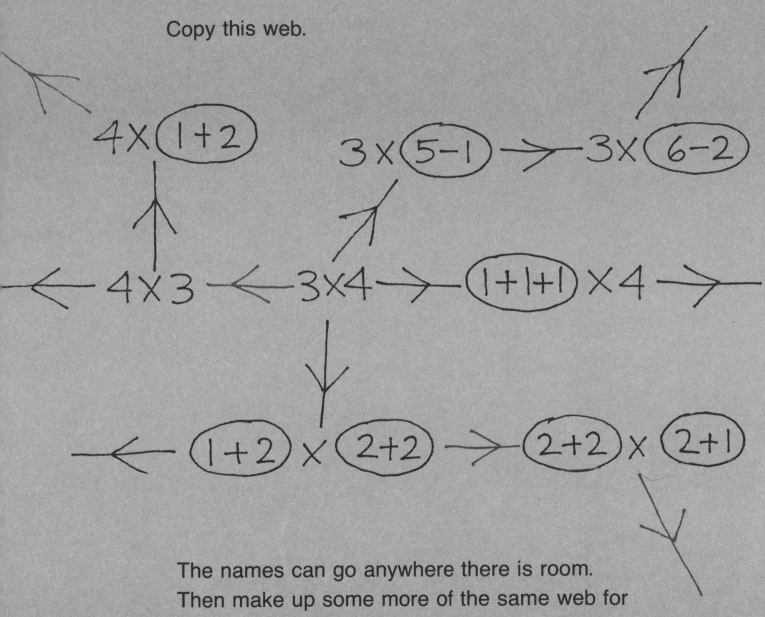

4 X (1+2)

3 × (5−1) → 3 × (6−2)

← 4×3 ← 3×4 → (1+1+1) × 4 →

← (1+2) × (2+2) → (2+2) × (2+1)

The names can go anywhere there is room.
Then make up some more of the same web for
yourself.

Ordinary wooden tables, like the one you probably have in your kitchen, can be of different sizes and shapes. So can multiplication tables! There are small ones:

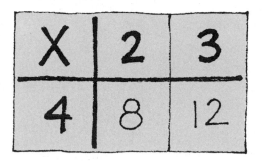

and rectangular ones:

X	1	2	3	4	5	6	7	8	9	10
1	1	2	3	4	5	6	7	8	9	10
2	2	4	6	8	10	12	14	16	18	20

circular tables:

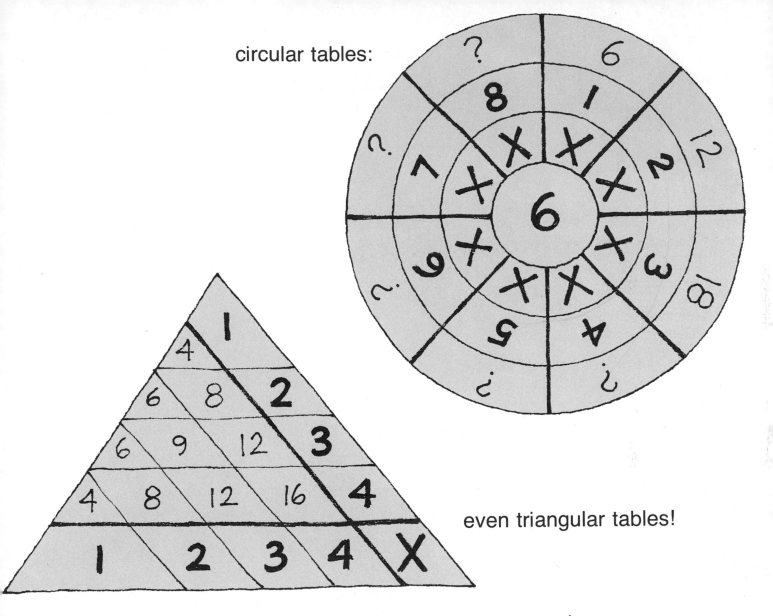

even triangular tables!

Make up some of your own, or copy these
and make them larger with more numbers.

We called **3 × 4** a product. **2 × 3 × 4** is a
TRIPLE PRODUCT. Its common name is **24**. Check
this, if you need to, by using stones.

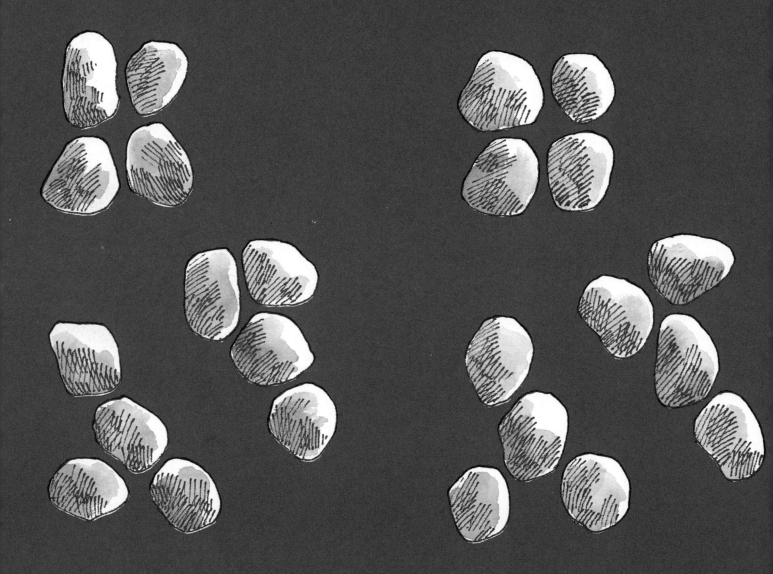

You can build tables of triple products. Put
each table on a stiff piece of cardboard.

Start with this:

2X	1	2	3	4	5	
1	2×1×1	2×1×2	2×1×3	2×1×4	2×1×5	2
2	2×2×1	2×2×2	2×2×3	2×2×4	2×2×5	2
3	2×3×1	2×3×2	2×3×3	2×3×4	2×3×5	
4	2×4×1	2×4×2	2×4×3	2×4×4	2×4×5	2

Then substitute for every triple product its common name.

2X	1	2	3	4	5	
1	2	4	6	8	10	
2	4	8	12	16	20	
3	6	12	18	24	30	
4	8	16	24	32	40	

You can make the table any size you like!

Make another card. This time every product
begins with "three times":

3X	1	2	3	4	5	
1	3×1×1	3×1×2	3×1×3	3×1×4	3×1×5	3
2	3×2×1	3×2×2	3×2×3	3×2×4	3×2×5	3

Again, change every product to its common name.

3X	1	2	3	4	5	
1	3	6	9	12	15	

Work each time with headings **I, 2, 3, 4, 5, 6**—or
further. The next card will have every product
beginning with **4 ×**, and the next with **5 ×**.

4X	1	2	3	4	5	
I	4×1×1	4×1×2	4×1×3	4×1×4	4×1×5	4
2	4×2×1	4×2×2	4×2×3	4×2×4	4×2×5	4

5X	1	2	3	4	5	
I	5×1×1	5×1×2	5×1×3	5×1×4	5×1×5	5
2	5×2×1	5×2×2	5×2×3	5×2×4	5×2×5	5

Go on building tables until you have the card where each product begins with "five times." Or go further.

10X	1	2	3	4	5	6	
1	10	20	30	40	50	60	70
2	20	40	60	80	100	120	140
3	30	60	90	120	150	180	210
4	40	80	120	160	200	240	280
5	50	100	150	200	250	300	350

Hang the cards on a string across the room.

You now have a simple COMPUTER. If you want to find the common name for a triple product— **2 × 5 × 4**, for instance—you can look at Card 2 and use the headings **5** and **4**. There's the answer— in the table!

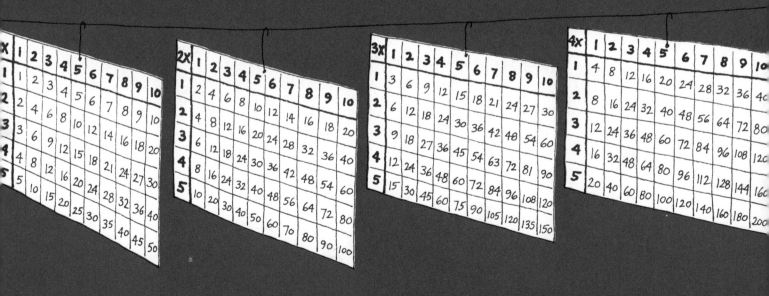

See if you can find *six* places on the cards where the common name for **2 × 5 × 4** can be found!

X	1	2	3	4	5	6	7	8	9	10
1	5	10	15	20	25	30	35	40	45	50
2	10	20	30	40	50	60	70	80	90	100
3	15	30	45	60	75	90	105	120	135	150
4	20	40	60	80	100	120	140	160	180	200
5	25	50	75	100	125	150	175	200	225	250

6X	1	2	3	4	5	6	7	8	9	10
1	6	12	18	24	30	36	42	48	54	60
2	12	24	36	48	60	72	84	96	108	120
3	18	36	54	72	90	108	126	144	162	180
4	24	48	72	96	120	144	168	192	216	240
5	30	60	90	120	150	180	210	240	270	300

7X	1	2	3	4	5	6	7	8	9	10
1	7	14	21	28	35	42	49	56	63	70
2	14	28	42	56	70	84	98	112	126	140
3	21	42	63	84	105	126	147	168	189	210
4	28	56	84	112	140	168	196	224	252	280
5	35	70	105	140	175	210	245	280	315	350

8X	1	2	3	4
1	8	16	24	32
2	16	32	48	6
3	24	48	72	96
4	32	64	96	12
5	40	80	120	16

ABOUT THE AUTHOR

John V. Trivett has been associated with innovative teaching of mathematics for many years—in England as Chairman of the Association of Teachers of Math, in the United States with the University of Illinois Arithmetic Project and the Madison Project, and as consultant to schools and universities from Florida to Alaska.

His special interest is "how children can learn math masterfully, creatively, and joyfully."

Presently a professor in the Faculty of Education at Simon Fraser University in Canada, Mr. Trivett lives in West Vancouver with his daughters and his wife—who is the author of *Shadow Geometry,* another Young Math Book.

ABOUT THE ILLUSTRATOR

Giulio Maestro was born in New York City and studied at the Cooper Union Art School and Pratt Graphics Center. Aside from picture-book illustration, he is well known for his beautiful hand lettering and his book jacket design. He enjoys etching and painting in his free time.

Mr. Maestro lives in Madison, Connecticut.